Let's Make Oatmeal

40 Oat-rageously Oat-standing Recipes

BY

Christina Tosch

Copyright Notes

Table of Contents

Introduction

If you aren't a fan of high fiber oatmeal, you will be now!

But before you discover the Let's Make Oatmeal collection of 40 oat-rageously oat-standing recipes read on and find out some fascinating facts!

- It was the Greeks who first made oats into porridge
- Every year, on October 28 the nation says Let's Make Oatmeal when it celebrates National Oatmeal Day

- Oatmeal can add flavor and texture to soups, smoothies and even burgers
- More oats are grown in Iowa than any other place in the USA
- A bowl of oatmeal can keep you feeling fuller for longer
- Oats not only help reduce the risk of heart disease but are also great for making sure you have healthy hair, nails, and skin
- Around 75 percent of US households have oatmeal in their kitchen cupboard

Sweet, savory, warm or chilled oatmeal is one of the best ever, go-to kitchen cupboard staples.

What are you waiting for? Let's Make Oatmeal!

Savory Oatmeal

Bacon and Mushroom Oatmeal

Breakfast, brunch, lunch or dinner, no problem when you can dish up this savory oatmeal from pot to plate in half an hour.

Servings: 1

Total Time: 30mins

Ingredients:

- Nonstick cooking spray
- ¼ cup mushrooms (sliced)
- 1 cup kale
- ⅓ cup rolled oats
- 1 egg
- ⅓ cup low-fat Greek yogurt
- Pinch of salt
- 3 rashers of bacon (cooked, crumbled)
- Pinch of red pepper flakes

Directions:

1. Heat a frying pan over moderate-high heat and spritz with nonstick cooking spray.

2. Add the mushrooms and kale to the pan and sauté for 2-3 minutes, until the kale begins to wilt and mushrooms are tender.

3. Cook the oatmeal according to the package directions.

4. Poach the egg.

5. Add the oatmeal to a bowl along with the yogurt and a pinch of salt.

6. Fold in the crumbled bacon, kale and mushrooms and evenly combine.

7. Top with the egg, and season with crushed red pepper.

8. Serve and enjoy.

Beef and Oatmeal Soup

Quick-cook oats give a basic soup great texture. So next time you are looking for a bowl of comfort food, reach for this oat-standing recipe.

Servings: 6

Total Time: 35mins

Ingredients:

- ¾ pound beef top sirloin (diced)
- 1 onion (peeled, chopped)
- 2 tbsp olive oil
- 2 carrots (peeled, sliced)
- 2 stalks of celery (chopped)
- 3 garlic cloves (peeled, finely chopped)
- 5 cups beef broth
- 1 (14 ounce) can diced tomatoes (drained)
- 2 bay leaves
- 4 sprigs of fresh thyme
- ½ cup quick-cook oats
- Salt and black pepper

Directions:

1. In a pan over moderate-high heat, brown the beef, and onion in the olive oil. Season.

2. Next, add the carrots followed by the celery and garlic. Continue to cook for an additional couple of minutes.

3. Pour in the broth and add the tomatoes followed by the bay leaves, and fresh thyme sprigs.

4. Bring the mixture to boil before reducing the heat to simmer. Cook until the veggies are bite tender, for 15-20 minutes.

5. Stir in the oats and simmer for an additional 3-5 minutes.

6. Remove and discard the sprigs of thyme and the bay leaves.

7. Taste, and adjust the seasoning as necessary.

Cheesy Shrimp Oatmeal

A deliciously filling oatmeal with melting Cheddar cheese, salty bacon, and tender shrimp is just the pick me up you need!

Servings: 2

Total Time: 20mins

Ingredients:

- 2 rashers of thick-cut bacon
- 2 cloves of garlic (peeled, minced)
- 8 medium-size fresh shrimp (shelled, deveined)
- Sea salt and freshly ground black pepper (to taste)
- 2 servings of unsweetened steel-cut oatmeal
- ⅔ cup mature Cheddar cheese (grated)
- Chives (chopped, to garnish)

Directions:

1. Add the bacon to a cold saucepan and over low to medium heat, slowly cook.

2. Once the bacon begins to curl, flip it over and cook on the reverse side.

3. Continue to cook and flip the bacon over, until it is brown and crisp all over.

4. Transfer the bacon to a paper towel-line plate to cool and set the bacon fat to one side to cook the shrimp.

5. Add 1 tbsp of the bacon fat to the pan and place over medium heat.

6. When the fat is sufficiently hot, add the garlic and cook for 30 seconds.

7. Add the shrimp and season.

8. Cook for between 45-60 seconds on one side until the shrimp starts to become pink. Flip over and cook until pink, for an additional 45-60 seconds.

9. Take the pan off the heat.

10. Put the oatmeal in a microwave-safe bowl and microwave for a couple of minutes, until warm.

11. Stir in the grated cheese, while stirring to combine entirely.

12. Transfer the oatmeal to a bowl, season to taste, garnish with chopped chives and enjoy.

Chicken and Miso Oatmeal

Oatmeal isn't just for breakfast, and this recipe makes great use of leftover chicken.

Servings: 2

Total Time: 25mins

Ingredients:

- 3 cups water
- 1 cup unflavored soy milk
- 1 cup steel-cut oats
- 1-3 tbsp miso (to taste)
- 4 ounces cooked leftover chicken breast

Directions:

1. Add the water, milk, and oats to a pan and set on high heat and stir.

2. As soon as the liquid boils, reduce the heat to moderate-low and occasionally stir to prevent the oats from sticking to the pan.

3. While the liquid boils, add the miso, allowing it to dissolve entirely.

4. After 12-15 minutes, add the cooked chicken and simmer for an additional 2-3 minutes before serving.

Cottage Cheese Oatmeal

Add protein to a bowl of oatmeal with a delicious bowl of oatmeal.

Servings: 1

Total Time: 15mins

Ingredients:

- ½ cup old fashioned oats
- ½ banana (peeled, sliced)
- Pinch of sea salt
- 1¼ cups water
- ½ tsp cinnamon
- ½ tsp vanilla essence
- ¼ cup cottage cheese

Directions:

1. In a pan, combine the oats with the banana, and salt. Pour in the water and stir to incorporate.

2. Add the cinnamon followed by the vanilla essence and a pinch of salt. Over moderate to high heat, heat for 8-10 minutes, until the majority of the liquid is absorbed. It is important to stir the oats 5-6 times, to make sure that the banana melts into the oats.

3. The oatmeal is ready when the liquid is absorbed, and the oats are fluffy and thick.

4. Remove the oats from the heat and gently stir in the cottage cheese. It is best, to begin with, ¼ cup and add more if needed.

5. Serve the oatmeal with your favorite toppings.

Curry Cashew Oatmeal

If you a craving a late-night supper then this curry and cashew oatmeal is perfect.

Servings: 1

Total Time: 20mins

Ingredients:

- 1 cup water
- Pinch of salt
- ½ cup old fashioned rolled oats
- 3 tbsp golden raisins
- 3 tbsp toasted cashews (chopped)
- ¼ tsp curry powder

Directions:

1. In a pan, bring the water and salt to boil.

2. Stir in the oats and turn the heat down to moderate and cook, while occasionally stirring until the majority of the liquid is absorbed, for 5 minutes.

3. Remove the pan from the heat, cover and allow to rest for 2-3 minutes.

4. Top with golden raisins, toasted cashews and a sprinkling of curry powder.

Mexican Oatmeal

If you are looking for something special, then Mexican oatmeal will tick all the boxes. It has taste, color, and texture.

Servings: 1

Total Time: 15mins

Ingredients:

- 1 tsp oil
- 2 cloves of garlic (peeled, minced)
- ¾ cup quick-cook oats
- ½ tsp taco seasoning
- ¼ tsp paprika
- ½ tsp freshly squeezed lime juice
- 2 cups water
- Salt (to season)

Toppings:

- Corn
- Salsa
- Cheddar cheese (grated)
- Avocado (peeled, pitted, mashed)
- Jalapeno peppers

Directions:

1. In a pot, heat the oil and add the garlic. Cook the garlic for 15 seconds until it emits its fragrance.

2. Add the oats followed by the taco seasoning, paprika, fresh lime juice, water, and salt. Mix thoroughly to combine and bring to boil.

3. Simmer for 3 minutes, until the oats are cooked through and the mixture has thickened. This will take 3-4 minutes. You may need to add a drop more water to achieve your preferred consistency.

4. Serve the oatmeal topped with corn, salsa, grated cheese, avocado, and jalapeno peppers.

5. Serve and enjoy.

Oatmeal with Greens and Yogurt

A toasted oat and nut topping is the crowning glory to a delicious bowl of oatmeal.

Servings: 1

Total Time: 30mins

Ingredients:

Topping:

- ¼ cup oats
- ¼ cup slivered raw almonds
- ¼ cup pumpkin seeds
- ¼ cup sunflower seeds
- ¼ tsp salt
- 1 tsp extra-virgin olive oil

Oatmeal:

- 1 cup water
- ½ cup oats
- Salt and freshly ground black pepper
- 1 tbsp extra-virgin olive oil
- 1 small clove garlic (peeled, finely diced)
- Pinch of crushed red pepper
- 5 ounces spinach leaves (washed, drained)
- Plain full-fat yogurt (to serve)

Directions:

1. Preheat the main oven to 350 degrees F.

2. For the topping, in a bowl, combine the oats with the almonds, pumpkin seeds, sunflower seeds, salt, and oil.

3. Transfer the mixture to a baking sheet and bake in the preheated oven for 10 minutes, until lightly toasted

4. for the oatmeal. In a pan, bring one cup of water to boil before adding the oats along with a pinch of salt. Turn the heat down to a low simmer and cover. Cook for 20 minutes, while occasionally stirring. Turn the heat off, cover the pan and steam for an additional 10 minutes.

5. In the meantime, prepare the greens — heat approximately 1 tbsp of oil in a skillet over moderate-high heat.

6. As soon as the oil begins to shimmer, add the garlic along with the red pepper. The garlic needs to simmer rather than brown.

7. Add the spinach and salt to taste. Allow to wilt for 60 seconds and turn over to cook evenly.

8. Put the oatmeal in a bowl, surround it with spinach and the juices from the pan. Garnish with approximately 1 tbsp of the toasted oat and nut topping.

9. Add a dollop of yogurt to the top and sprinkle with ground pepper, salt and a drizzle of oil.

10. Enjoy.

One-Pot Salmon and Oatmeal Hash

Oatmeal gets a gourmet makeover with salmon and lots of veggies – enjoy!

Servings: 2

Total Time: 20mins

Ingredients:

- Nonstick cooking spray
- ½ yellow onion (peeled, chopped)
- ¼ cup uncooked steel-cut oats
- 1 cup boiling water
- 1 cup cauliflower florets (finely chopped)
- 1 large zucchini (chopped)
- 8 ounces cooked salmon
- Dried dill (to taste)
- Salt (to season)

Directions:

1. Spritz a large pan with nonstick cooking spray. Add the onion to the pan and cook along with the oats for a couple of minutes, on moderate heat, while continually stirring.

2. Pour the boiling water into the oat-onion mixture.

3. Add the cauliflower and zucchini, simmer for approximately 15 minutes, until the mixture slightly thickens.

4. Remove the oats from the heat and allow to stand for a few minutes to thicken.

5. Stir in the salmon, dill and season with salt.

6. Serve.

Parmesan and Pea Oatmeal with Mint and Lemon

This Italian-style oatmeal is sure to become your secret guilty pleasure.

Servings: 1

Total Time: 25mins

Ingredients:

- ¾ tbsp butter
- 1 shallot (diced)
- ⅔ cup steel cut quick oats
- 1 cup frozen or fresh peas
- 2 cups chicken stock
- ¼ cup Parmesan cheese (freshly grated)
- 1 tbsp fresh lemon zest
- ¼ cup mint leaves (finely shredded)
- Salt and black pepper

Directions:

1. In a pan, melt the butter.

2. Add the shallot and cook for a few minutes.

3. Next, add the oats and occasionally stir over low heat for between 3-4 minutes, until the oats and shallots are toasted, golden and fragrant.

4. Add the peas and pour in the stock, stirring to combine.

5. Continue to cook and stir for 3-5 minutes, until the mixture thickens.

6. Stir in the grated cheese, lemon zest, and shredded mint.

7. Season to taste and enjoy.

Savory Tomato Oatmeal

This savory oatmeal makes a great snack for any time of day or night. It's fast, inexpensive, and family-friendly.

Servings: 4

Total Time: 15mins

Ingredients:

- 1 cup whole grain rolled oats
- 1 tbsp olive oil
- 1 cup cherry tomatoes (halved)
- Salt and black pepper (to season)

Directions:

1. Prepare the oats according to the package directions. Set to one side.

2. Over a moderate flame, in a large skillet, add the oil and heat until hot.

3. Next, add the halved tomatoes and season with salt and black pepper.

4. Cook for several minutes on each side and remove from the heat.

5. Serve the oatmeal topped with the blistered tomatoes.

6. Serve and enjoy.

Spicy Thai Peanut Savory Oatmeal

This Asian-inspired oatmeal recipe is sure to have everyone coming back for more, and more, and more.

Servings: 2

Total Time: 25mins

Ingredients:

- 2 cups old fashioned oats
- 2 cups chicken stock
- 1 cup coconut milk
- 2 tsp fresh ginger (peeled, minced)
- 1 garlic clove (peeled, minced)
- ½-1 tsp dried Thai chilies (crushed)
- 1 tsp soy sauce
- 1 tsp rice vinegar
- 2 scallions (chopped)
- ¼ cup roasted peanuts (for topping)

Directions:

1. In a pan, combine the oats with the chicken stock, milk, ginger, garlic, and dried chilies.

2. Over moderately high heat, heat to a simmer.

3. Turn the heat down to low and while covered, simmer the oatmeal for 5 minutes. It is important to stir the oatmeal during cooking occasionally.

4. As soon as the mixture is thickened, remove it for the heat and stir in the soy sauce and vinegar.

5. Top the oatmeal with scallions and peanuts.

6. Enjoy.

Turmeric and Chickpea Oats

Turmeric has great anti-inflammatory properties, which makes it a great addition to any meal, any time of the day.

Servings: 1

Total Time: 15mins

Ingredients:

- ½ cup rolled oats
- ½ cup unsweetened soy or almond milk
- ½ cup water
- Pinch salt
- Pinch black pepper
- 1 cup baby spinach (rinsed, squeeze dried, chopped)
- ¼-½ tsp turmeric (to taste)
- 1 tbsp nutritional yeast
- 1 tbsp tahini (to serve)
- Cashews (chopped, to serve)
- ⅓ cup cooked chickpeas

Directions:

1. The night before, add the oats, almond milk, water, salt and black pepper to a pan. Cover and place in the fridge, overnight.

2. The following day, in the pan, bring the oats to boil.

3. While the oats boil, turn the heat down to a simmer.

4. Place the baby spinach on top of the oats, cover the pan with a lid and allow the spinach to wilt.

5. Once the spinach has wilted, stir it into the oats, to entirely combine.

6. Next, add the turmeric starting with ¼ tsp (to taste).

7. Cook the oats while frequently stirring, until creamy and thick. This will take 2-3 minutes.

8. Stir in the yeast, add additional salt and pepper, to taste, along with the tahini and chopped cashews.

9. Top with chickpeas and enjoy.

Venison Steak n' Egg Oatmeal

Juicy venison and freshly fried eggs on top of creamy oatmeal; what's not to like?

Servings: 2

Total Time: 40mins

Ingredients:

- 1½ cups water
- ½ cup steel cut oats
- Salt
- 1 (¼ pound) venison steak
- 2 tbsp butter
- 2 eggs
- ¼ cup red wine vinegar
- Salt and black pepper (to season)

Directions:

1. In a pan, bring the water to boil. Add the oats along with the salt and turn down to a simmer. Cook until tender, for approximately 20-30 minutes.

2. Cook the venison to your preference in a pan. Set aside to rest before slicing into ¼" thick pieces. Cooking times are approximately 6 minutes for medium-rare, and 7-8 minutes for medium.

3. In the meantime, over moderate heat, heat the butter in a pan.

4. Fry the eggs to your preferred level of doneness.

5. Divide the oatmeal between 2 bowls.

6. Arrange the eggs on top of the oatmeal, leaving any leftover butter in the pan.

7. Add the vinegar and allow to reduce slightly.

8. Season with salt, black pepper and serve.

Sweet Oatmeal

Baklava Oatmeal

A Greek breakfast may very well consist of coffee and dare we say it a cigarette, but that doesn't mean that you can't start the day off in style with this delicious oatmeal.

Servings: 4

Total Time: 25mins

Ingredients:

- 1 tbsp butter
- 1½ cups walnuts (roughly chopped)
- 1 tsp cinnamon
- Pinch of ground cloves
- Pinch of salt
- ½ cup raisins
- 6 tbsp Greek honey
- 2 cups quick-cook oats
- 6 cups milk

Directions:

1. Over moderate heat, in a frying pan, melt the butter.

2. Add the walnuts to the hot pan and over moderate heat, stir for 3 minutes.

3. Stir in ½ tsp of cinnamon, a pinch of cloves, a pinch of salt and move them around the pan for 60 seconds, to allow them to release their fragrance.

4. Stir in the raisins along with 2 tbsp of honey.

5. Continue to cook until the walnuts are just caramelized, for an additional 2-3 minutes.

6. While the walnuts are caramelizing, prepare the oatmeal: In a pan, combine the oatmeal with the milk and while occasionally stirring cook over moderate heat, until the oatmeal thickens to your preferred consistency.

7. Divide the oatmeal between 4 plates, and scatter with the walnut and raisin mixture.

8. Sprinkle over the remaining cinnamon and pour over the leftover honey. Serve.

Butterscotch Oatmeal

Sweet and filling, this butterscotch oatmeal is 'oat of this world.'

Servings: 3-4

Total Time: 20mins

Ingredients:

- 1¾ cups milk
- ½ cup packed brown sugar
- 1 egg (lightly beaten)
- 1 cup quick-cooking oats
- 1 tbsp butter

Directions:

1. In a pan over moderate heat, combine the milk with the sugar and lightly beaten egg.

2. Cook, while constantly stirring for 5-6 minutes, or until the mixture comes to boil.

3. Add the oats and cook while stirring for 60 seconds.

4. Remove the pan from the heat and add the butter. Cover with a lid and set aside for 3-5 minutes.

Caramelized Pear Oatmeal

Warm, sweet, and oat-rageously oat-standing!

Servings: 2

Total Time: 20mins

Ingredients:

- 1 cup hearty cut oatmeal
- 2 tbsp ground flaxseed
- 2 tsp coconut oil
- 2 tbsp pure maple syrup
- 1 ripe pear (peeled, pitted, diced)
- 1 tsp ground cinnamon
- Nut butter (to serve)

Directions:

1. Prepare the oatmeal according to the package instructions.

2. Stir the ground flaxseed into the cooked oatmeal.

3. In a skillet, heat the coconut oil along with the maple syrup over moderate heat, and cook until bubbling.

4. Fold in the pears together with the cinnamon. Cover with a lid and steam for 10 minutes, until the pears are softened. Take the lid off and cook for a few more minutes to caramelize the pears.

5. Spoon the oatmeal into 2 bowls and top with diced pears and nut butter.

Carrot Cake Oatmeal

Your favourite cake flavor reinvented as sweet and spiced oatmeal, what's not to love?!

Servings: 1

Total Time: 10mins

Ingredients:

- 1 medium-size carrot (peeled, grated)
- 1 cup water
- Pinch of salt
- ½ cup rolled oats
- ¼ tsp vanilla essence
- ⅛ tsp cinnamon
- 1 tbsp raisins
- 1 tbsp brown sugar
- 1 tbsp butter
- 2 tbsp walnuts

Directions:

1. Add the grated carrot peel to a pan along with 1 cup of water and a pinch of salt. Over high heat, bring to boil.

2. Stir in the oats, vanilla essence, cinnamon, and raisins. Adjust the heat to a simmer, and cook, while frequently stirring for 5 minutes, or until the oats and carrots are tender.

3. Remove the pan from the heat and stir in the brown sugar.

4. Transfer the mixture to a bowl.

5. Dot the oatmeal with bits of butter and scatter with additional brown sugar.

6. Top with walnuts and enjoy.

Cherry Pie Oatmeal Bowl

Enjoy before work, after-school, or at suppertime, this oatmeal really is as sweet as cherry pie.

Servings: 1-2

Total Time: 12mins

Ingredients:

- 2 cups water
- ⅔ cup dry oats
- 1 cup cherries (washed, pitted, halved)
- 2 dates (pitted, chop into small pieces)
- 2 tsp cinnamon
- 1 tsp vanilla extract
- 1-2 tbsp tahini
- 2 tbsp ground flaxseed
- Pecans (to serve)

Directions:

1. In a pan, bring the water to boil. Add the oats and reduce the heat.

2. Add the cherries along with the dates, cinnamon, vanilla extract, and tahini.

3. Allow the oats to simmer for 2-3 minutes, frequently stirring to prevent the oats from burning.

4. Stir in the ground flaxseed just before stirring.

5. Garnish with pecans and enjoy.

Coconut-Lime Breakfast Oatmeal

Coconut and lime have long been the perfect pairing, and when combined with creamy oatmeal and macadamia nuts, we are sure they won't disappoint.

Servings: 1

Total Time: 5mins

Ingredients:

- 1 cup water
- ½ cup rolled oats
- 2 tsp coconut cream concentrate
- Pinch of salt
- 1 tsp freshly squeezed lime juice
- 2 tbsp dried coconut
- ½ tsp lime zest
- ¼ cup macadamia nuts
- Honey (to serve)

Directions:

1. In a pan, combine the water with the oats, coconut concentrate, and a pinch of salt. Bring to boil and simmer while stirring for a couple of minutes.

2. Remove the pan from the heat, and stir in the lime juice, dried coconut, and lime zest.

3. Top with the macadamia nuts and drizzle with honey.

4. Enjoy.

Honey, Date and Pine Nut Oatmeal

How do you like your oatmeal in the morning?

Servings: 1

Total Time: 17mins

Ingredients:

- Pinch of salt
- 1 cup water
- ½ cup old-fashioned rolled oats
- 1 tsp honey
- 2 tbsp dates (pitted, chopped)
- 1 tbsp pine nuts (toasted)
- ¼ tsp ground cinnamon

Directions:

1. In a pan, bring the salt and water to boil.

2. Stir in the rolled oats, turn the heat down to moderate and cook while occasionally stirring until the majority of the liquid is absorbed, for approximately 5 minutes.

3. Remove the pan from the heat, cover with a lid, and allow to stand for 2-3 minutes.

4. Top the oatmeal with honey, dates, pine nuts and a sprinkling of ground cinnamon.

Mocha Oatmeal

Start the day, the healthy way with this coffee and oatmeal breakfast – guaranteed to keep you going until lunchtime.

Servings: 2

Total Time: 8mins

Ingredients

- 1 banana (peeled, mashed)
- ¾ cup oats
- ¼ tsp salt
- 1 tsp instant coffee
- ½ tsp cacao powder
- 1 tsp honey
- ¼ cup walnuts
- 1 cup water
- 1 cup milk

Directions:

1. Add the banana, oats, salt, coffee, cacao powder, honey, and walnuts to a pan on moderate heat.

2. Add the water, and simmer until a thickened consistency.

3. Transfer to a bowl and add the milk, stirring to combine.

4. Enjoy.

Pumpkin Pie Oatmeal

Winter, come summer or fall, all you need is a bowl of pumpkin pie oatmeal.

Servings: 4

Total Time: 12mins

Ingredients:

- 1 cup old-fashioned rolled oats
- 1¾ cups almond milk
- ¼ cup pumpkin puree
- ½ tsp vanilla extract
- ½ tsp ground cinnamon
- ¼ tsp ground nutmeg
- ½ cup pecans (chopped)
- ¼ cup pure maple syrup

Directions:

1. In a pan, over moderate heat, combine the oats with the milk and bring to boil. Turn the heat down to a simmer and while occasionally stirring, cook for 3-5 minutes, until you achieve your desired consistency.

2. Stir in the pumpkin puree followed by the vanilla extract, cinnamon, and nutmeg until heated through for 60 seconds.

3. Serve, garnished with chopped pecans and maple syrup.

Slow-Cooked Nectarine Oatmeal

Nectarines make a juicy-licious oatmeal ingredient. So next time you go to your local farmer's market, why not pick up a bag?

Servings: 1

Total Time: 35mins

Ingredients:

- ⅓ cup rolled oatmeal
- ½ nectarine (pitted, chopped)
- ⅛ tsp cake spice
- ⅛ tsp vanilla essence
- Pinch of salt
- ⅔ cup unsweetened almond milk
- ½ tbsp light brown sugar
- Almond milk (to serve, optional)

Directions:

1. Preheat the main oven to 350 degrees F.

2. In a bowl, combine the oatmeal with the nectarines, cake spice, vanilla essence, salt, and almond milk.

3. Transfer the mixture to a ramekin dish.

4. Sprinkle light brown sugar over the top and place in the preheated oven for half an hour.

5. Serve hot, with a splash of chilled almond milk.

Sweet Potato Oatmeal

Switch up your regular bowl of oatmeal with sweet potato, maple syrup, and cinnamon. Sprinkle over your favorite toppings and enjoy.

Servings: 2

Total Time: 1hour 20mins

Ingredients

- 1 medium-size sweet potato
- 1 cup rolled oats
- 1 cup water
- ½ cup unflavored milk
- Pure maple syrup (to taste)
- Dash of nutmeg
- 1 tsp cinnamon
- 2 tsp chia seeds (to serve)
- ½ cup raisins (to serve)
- ½ cup pecans (chopped, to serve)

Directions:

1. First, pierce the potato 3-4 times.

2. Bake the potato at 400 degrees F for approximately 60 minutes, until softened.

3. Alternatively, in the microwave cook the potato for 5-10 minutes. When the potato is nearly finished cooking, prepare the oatmeal by mixing with the water and simmer on the stovetop for approximately 5 minutes. You may need to add a drop more water.

4. As soon as the potato is fork-tender, cut it open and scoop out its insides.

5. Add the potato to the oatmeal and with a fork, stir to break up any large chunks and create a smooth consistency.

6. Add the milk, maple syrup, nutmeg, and cinnamon, stir until incorporated.

7. Spoon into bowls and serve with a sprinkling of nutmeg, chia seeds, raisins, and pecans.

Vanilla and Coconut Oatmeal

This creamy bowl of oats smells as good as it tastes!

Servings: 1

Total Time: 15mins

Ingredients:

- 1 cup water
- ½ cup oatmeal
- Vanilla essence (to taste)
- ¼ cup unsweetened coconut (shredded)
- ½ banana (peeled, mashed)

Directions:

1. Pour the water into a bowl.

2. Stir in the oatmeal and cook for 6-8 minutes.

3. Stir in the vanilla essence. The amount will depend entirely on your preference.

4. When the oatmeal is nearly ready to serve, add the coconut along with the mashed banana. Cover the bowl with a lid and set aside for 5 minutes.

Drinks

Apple Oatmeal Smoothie

There is no better way to start the day than with a delicious apple and oatmeal smoothie.

Servings: 1

Total Time: 3mins

Ingredients:

- 1 medium-size green apple (peeled, cored, and diced)
- ¼ cup plain Greek yogurt
- ¼ cup quick cook oats
- 1 cup almond milk

Directions:

1. Add the apple, yogurt, oats, and milk to a food blender and process to your preferred consistency.

2. Serve.

Apricot Oatmeal Smoothie

Lots of healthy ingredients go into this smoothie, making it the perfect after-school snack.

Servings: 2

Total Time: 6mins

Ingredients:

- ¼ cup dry quick rolled oats
- ½ cup water
- 4 whole velvet apricots (pitted)
- 1 small banana (peeled)
- 1 tbsp hemp seeds
- ½ tbsp goji berries
- 1 tbsp raw peanuts
- 1 tbsp walnuts (chopped)
- 2 cups flax milk
- ½ tsp raw honey

Directions:

1. In a bowl, combine the oats with the water. Microwave for 60 seconds. Remove from the microwave and set aside to cool.

2. Meanwhile, in a food blender, combine the apricots, banana, hemp seeds, goji berries, peanuts, walnuts, flax milk and raw honey, and process until silky smooth.

3. Finally, combine the cool oatmeal into the mixture and blend once more for 30 seconds.

4. Pour into glasses and serve.

Atholl Brose

Not for the faint-hearted, this boozy oat-based drink is a New Year's Eve Scottish favorite.

Servings: 2

Total Time: 24 hours 10mins

Ingredients:

- ½ cup steel cut oats
- 1½ cups water
- 3 tsp heather honey
- 8 ounces whiskey
- 5 ounces heavy cream

Directions:

1. Prepare the oats by soaking them in water for 24 hours.

2. Drain the brose (thin porridge) from the oats.

3. Line a strainer with paper towels and squeeze the remaining liquid out of the oats using a linen cloth.

4. Using a metal spoon, stir in the honey.

5. Pour in the whiskey and stir to combine.

6. Stir in the cream and serve.

Date, Oat and Banana Smoothie

Start the day with a healthy oat smoothie, and you will be good to go until lunchtime.

Servings: 2

Total Time:

Ingredients:

- 1 cup oats (roasted)
- 1½ cups milk (divided)
- ½ cup dates (seeded)
- 1 banana (peeled)
- 1 tbsp honey
- Pinch of cinnamon
- 1 tbsp fresh cream

Directions:

1. In a bowl, combine the oats with half of the milk, until softened.

2. Transfer to a food blender along with dates, banana, honey, cinnamon, and remaining milk, blend to incorporate.

3. Add the cream, blend, and enjoy.

Healthy Oat Tea

Tea without the tea! This hot beverage is believed to be great for relieving colds and is said to help strengthen the immune system.

Servings: 4

Total Time: 35mins

Ingredients:

- 2 tbsp rolled oats
- 1 cinnamon stick
- 4 cups water
- 1 tbsp honey (to taste)
- 2 tsp vanilla essence

Directions:

1. Add the oats, cinnamon stick, and water to a pan. Bring to boil before reducing the heat to a simmer, while covered, for half an hour.

2. Turn the heat off and stir in the honey followed by the vanilla.

3. Strain the mixture to remove the oats.

4. Serve and enjoy.

Healthy Pumpkin Oatmeal Shake

If you are watching your weight, then this shake will tick all the boxes. It is packed with lots of minerals, vitamins, antioxidants, and flavor!

Servings: 4

Total Time: 4mins

Ingredients:

- ½ cup quick oats
- 2 cups water
- 1 cup almond milk
- ½ cup canned pumpkin puree
- 3 tbsp brown sugar
- 1 tsp cinnamon
- Pumpkin pie spice (to taste)
- 1 cup ice

Directions:

1. In a pan, cook the oats along with the water for 1-2 minutes, while frequently stirring until bubbly and thick.

2. Remove the pan from the heat and set aside to cool.

3. In a food blender, combine the milk with the pumpkin puree, brown sugar, cinnamon, and pie spice.

4. Add the oats along with the ice and on high, blend until silky smooth.

5. Transfer to the fridge to chill before serving.

Instant Oatmeal Coffee

Instant coffee with instant oatmeal, made in an instant is a great mid-morning boost.

Servings: 1

Total Time: 2min

Ingredients:

- 1 sachet instant coffee
- 6-7 teaspoons instant oatmeal
- Water (boiling, as needed)

Directions:

1. Pour the instant coffee into your favorite mug.

2. Add the oatmeal followed by sufficient boiling water to fill the mug.

3. Stir to combine.

4. Drink and enjoy.

Make-Ahead Vanilla Mint Oatmeal Smoothie

This minty smoothie is well worth the wait. Blend up a batch the night before and enjoy the following morning.

Servings: 1

Total Time: 8hours 5mins

Ingredients:

- ½ cup rolled oats
- ¾ cup unsweetened almond milk
- ½ tsp vanilla essence
- ½ cup baby spinach
- 1 ripe banana (peeled, frozen)
- 2 tbsp avocado
- 2-3 drops of mint essence
- ½ - 1 tbsp sweetener (to taste)

Directions:

1. The night before, combine the oats with the almond milk, and vanilla essence in a blender. Stir to incorporate, cover and transfer to the fridge, overnight.

2. The following day, take the blender jug out of the fridge and add the spinach along with the frozen banana and avocado.

3. On high, blend until you achieve a creamy smooth consistency.

4. If the smoothie is too thick, add a drop more milk.

5. Add a few drops of mint essence, to taste, and blend for an additional 2-3 seconds.

6. Sweeten to taste and serve.

Mexican Oatmeal Shake

Shake things up a little, with cinnamon and enjoy this south of the border shake.

Servings: 1

Total Time:

Ingredients:

- 1 cup water
- ⅔ cup milk
- 1 cup oats
- 1 tbsp ground cinnamon
- 1 tbsp runny honey
- Artificial sweetener (of choice, to taste)

Directions:

1. Combine the water, milk, oats, ground cinnamon, and honey in a food blender. Process for 30-60 seconds to fully incorporate.

2. Taste and sweeten a necessary.

Oatmeal Latte

Who needs an expensive coffee shop latte, when you can enjoy this easy-to-make pick-me-up at home?

Servings: 2

Total Time: 10mins

Ingredients:

- 1 cup old fashioned oats
- 2½ cups whole milk
- ¼ tsp salt
- ⅛ tsp cinnamon
- 1 tsp vanilla extract
- 3 tbsp brown sugar
- 2-4 shots of espresso
- Granola (to top)

Directions:

1. Add the oats along with 1½ cups of milk to a pan over moderate-low heat.

2. Add the salt followed by the cinnamon and stir well to combine.

3. Meanwhile, steam or froth the remaining cup of whole milk.

4. Add approximately ¾ cup of the frothy milk to the oats and cook while frequently stirring until the oats are creamy.

5. Remove the pan from the heat and stir in the remaining milk followed by the vanilla and sugar.

6. Top with a shot of espresso (to taste) and sprinkle with granola.

7. Enjoy!

Orange Creamsicle Oatmeal Smoothie

Say hello to a brand new day with this sweet and citrusy smoothie.

Servings: 1

Total Time: 8 hours 5mins

Ingredients:

- ⅓ cup rolled oats
- ½ cup freshly squeezed orange juice
- 1 orange (peeled, seeded, sliced)
- ½ tsp vanilla essence
- 1 ripe banana (peeled, frozen, sliced)

1-2 tsp maple syrup (to sweeten)

Directions:

1. The night before, combine the oats with the fresh orange juice, orange slice and vanilla essence in a food blender, stir and transfer to the fridge overnight.

2. The following day, remove the blender jug from the refrigerator and add the chunks of frozen banana.

3. On high, blend until a smooth consistency is achieved.

4. Sweeten to taste with maple syrup and enjoy.

Overnight Oat Cappuccino

In need of a caffeine hit? Then prepare this oaty cappuccino and get the best wake-up call, ever!

Servings: 1

Total Time: 8hours 5mins

Ingredients:

- ⅓ cup rolled oats
- 1 tsp chia seeds
- Pinch of cinnamon
- Pinch kosher salt
- ⅓ cup yogurt
- ½ cup strong coffee
- ⅓ cup milk

Directions:

1. In a jar, combine the oats with the chia seeds, cinnamon, kosher salt, plain yogurt, and coffee.

2. Chill in the fridge for at least 2 hours, or preferably overnight.

3. The following morning, froth the milk and pour on top.

4. Serve.

Pineapple and Coconut Oatmeal Smoothie

Enjoy this non-drinkers answer to a tropical pina colada.

Servings: 2

Total Time: 5mins

Ingredients:

- ¼ cup oatmeal
- 1 cup coconut milk (chilled)
- ¼ cup Greek yogurt
- 1 cup frozen pineapple chunks
- 1 tsp honey
- ⅓ tsp vanilla essence

Directions:

1. Add the oatmeal, coconut milk, Greek yogurt, pineapple chunks, honey and vanilla essence to a food blender, and process to your preferred consistency.

2. Serve and enjoy.

Salted Caramel Oatmeal Smoothie

If you like smoothies, you will love this recipe! Combining salted caramel with dates, and oatmeal, it really is a snack in a glass.

Servings: 2-3

Total Time: 5mins

Ingredients:

- 1 cup dates (pitted)
- 1 tbsp almond butter
- 3 cups unsweetened almond milk
- 1 tsp vanilla essence
- ½ cup cooked oatmeal
- Pinch of salt
- 10-12 marshmallows (to serve)

Directions:

1. In a food blender, combine the dates with the almond butter, almond milk, vanilla essence, oatmeal, and salt. Process until silky smooth.

2. Pour into chilled glasses, scatter mini mallows over the top and serve.

Author's Afterthoughts

I would like to express my deepest thanks to you, the reader, for making this investment in one my books. I cherish the thought of bringing the love of cooking into your home.

With so much choice out there, I am grateful you decided to Purch this book and read it from beginning to end.

Please let me know by submitting an Amazon review if you enjoyed this book and found it contained valuable information to help you in your culinary endeavors. Please take a few minutes to express your opinion freely and honestly. This will help others make an informed decision on purchasing and provide me with valuable feedback.

Thank you for taking the time to review!

Christina Tosch

About the Author

Christina Tosch is a successful chef and renowned cookbook author from Long Grove, Illinois. She majored in Liberal Arts at Trinity International University and decided to pursue her passion of cooking when she applied to the world renowned Le Cordon Bleu culinary school in Paris, France. The school was lucky to recognize the immense talent of this chef and she excelled in her courses, particularly Haute Cuisine. This skill was recognized and rewarded by several highly regarded Chicago restaurants, where she was offered the prestigious position of head chef.

Christina and her family live in a spacious home in the Chicago area and she loves to grow her own vegetables and herbs in the garden she lovingly cultivates on her sprawling estate. Her and her husband have two beautiful children, 3 cats, 2 dogs and a parakeet they call Jasper. When Christina is not hard at work creating beautiful meals for Chicago's elite, she is hard at work writing engaging e-books of which she has sold over 1500.

Make sure to keep an eye out for her latest books that offer helpful tips, clear instructions and witty anecdotes that will bring a smile to your face as you read!

Made in the USA
Coppell, TX
10 January 2020